Celebrity
scarves

Abra Edelman

Celebrity

scarves

introduction by isaac mizrahi

Abra Edelman

sixth&springbooks

Library of Congress Cataloging-in-Publication Data
Abra Edelman
        Celebrity scarves / Abra Edelman
                p. cm.
        ISBN 1-931543-27-5 Trade
        ISBN 1-931543-69-0 Paper
        1. Knitting—Patterns. 2. Scarves. 3. Celebrities—Clothing. I. Title.

        TT825.A25 2003
        746.43'20432--dc21   2003041569

Manufactured in China

1 3 5 7 9 10 8 6 4 2

First Edition

sixth&spring
books

233 Spring Street
New York, NY 10013

foreward

I have a confession: I am an "immediate gratification" junkie, which in knitting terms means that I love making scarves. To date, I have knit more than 300 scarves. Sweaters have no place in my gene pool; the truth is, I find concentrating on increasing, decreasing and counting much too stressful. For me, knitting is all about relaxation.

Because they are easy and inexpensive to make (except for those luscious cashmeres), scarves truly are a knitter's best friend. They reduce stress, provide constant entertainment and make beautiful and personal gifts. Everyone I know (and even those I don't know), from my two daughters to my manicurist to the conductor on the Amtrak from Boston to New York, has at least one of my scarves. And a scarf is a friend, not just to knitters but women in general; for a scarf will never judge or criticize you, nor will it care if you're a size 2 or a size 12. They always fit and work well with most ensembles, especially the ever-popular black outfit.

I learned to knit while visiting a movie set. One of the young actresses on the set was sitting next to me, knitting, and asked me if I would like to learn, to which I replied with a shrug, "Sure, why not?" Before long, I learned the basics and immediately fell in love with the craft—I was hooked. I graduated from potholders to scarves in one morning, and by the end of the week I was on my fourth scarf. I started with big needles (#15-35) and yarns that would hide my mistakes; I personally feel that you shouldn't be afraid of mistakes, since they only add to the personality of the scarf.

Along with knitting, I also love shopping—especially for yarn. I love the myriad textures, palettes and hands of all the yarns. Browsing a yarn store to mix-and-match eye-catching yarn combinations and to test out different needle sizes is like buying a dress and searching for the perfect shoes to match. I always leave the yarn store with enough yarn to make at least three or four scarves. After all, how often do you leave a boutique with just one pair of shoes?

When I first proposed the idea of doing a book that featured scarves knit by celebrities (since it was an actress who first taught me to knit), the publishing company loved the idea. Within a few months, we had our first photo shoot with Julianna Margulies. All the celebrities were very helpful, not only squeezing in a few moments to knit the scarves but also setting aside time for the photo shoots and donating the scarves for a charity auction to benefit amfAR.

The pages of this book brim with an array of amazing scarves, stitched with yarns of all colors, weights and textures. In addition, each scarf is accompanied by concise, easy-to-follow instructions. Whether you want to knit a scarf designed by Vanna White or Rosie Perez or use their designs to inspire your own work of art, *Celebrity Scarves* offers a fabulous collection of beautiful knits.

The variations of scarves and the reasons for making them are endless. In addition to being an ideal project for novice knitters, they've become one of the hottest accessories of recent years and allow the knitter to experiment with new color combinations and stitch techniques. Remember, there is no right way to knit a scarf. The most important aspect of knitting is to have fun. We hope you enjoy reading this book as much as we enjoyed working on it.

Abra

table
of contents

introduction

While some people have vivid memories of their first experience with knitting, I'm not sure exactly when I learned, though I have vague memories of my Aunt Norma teaching me. Don't ask me how I learned to ride a bike either; knitting is just one of those things.

I learned to knit and became a man simultaneously. I started knitting the same year that I got bar mitzvahed, which I always assumed meant something significant as it related to sweaters and manhood. I designed and made my first sweater: a lavender heather tweed crewneck with sleeves that were knit intentionally too long. Everyone thought it was cute that I had overknit the sleeves, when in fact it was just annoying to be misunderstood. So much for radical design ideas at 13.

In my experience, knitting is more about ripping

out and reknitting than anything else. Unless this is acknowledged, great knitting will never occur. It's important to realize that usually what you do will have to be redone, sometimes more than once. Knitting is a kind of Zen-like commitment, like a form of therapy, where the result is not the reason you engage; the pleasure you get in doing is much more important. A project can take any given length of time to finish. You need faith to be a knitter. You start without knowing what the end will bring, and after a while that becomes the greatest pleasure— the not knowing, the surprise, the true creativity that is constantly being tested.

On the other hand, knitting is like a bodily function; it just happens. Involuntary, like blinking or breathing—it's truly one of the great ways to relax. It's a form of meditation, which brings a great clarity of mind and spirit and a great sweater in the end.

What's better than a form of productive meditation? There's a lot of plain, mindless knitting to be done in-between all the intarsia and cabling and decreasing and popcorning—plain knitting that's both fully absorbing and mindless, like the equivalent of chanting to certain sects of monks. The other fancier stitching usually comes just in time to keep us from getting bored. Just when you're ready for a challenge, it's time to transfer to circular needles

Grandma isn't the only one knitting anymore; suddenly everyone's doing it. I've noticed that fabulous young starlettes are knitting. They've finally found the perfect thing to do on movie sets while waiting for their shots. Sarah Jessica Parker was working on a pretty blue-silver metallic scarf when I last visited her "Sex and the City" location trailer, and Lauren Ambrose brought her knitting to the set of "The Isaac Mizrahi Show," where we did a

segment about her enthusiasm for the craft. Not that one feels sorry for movie starlettes, but location trailers and dressing rooms can be pretty horrible places, and if you did feel a slight twinge of sympathy you might be really glad they found their way to scarf knitting to take their minds off their surroundings.

And it is scarf knitting specifically that's so useful to the Hollywood girls. Let's face it—there aren't many who could unwind or focus while trying to figure out a complicated Fair Isle cardigan or even a cable-front crewneck. But a scarf—a simple, straightforward muffler—makes for the perfect diversion, the perfect balm for one's nerves, the perfect thing to allay the boredom of memorizing lines, and even the perfect thing to return to after wrapping a shot.

Knitting a scarf can sometimes be simpler than wearing it. And sometimes the knitting, not the wearing of it, is the *raison d'être*. I know people who knit scarves to give them away as gifts, while others can never part with their work. You really have to do a little soul-searching these days before you decide which scarf to knit. In the past, there were trends that made it easier. Now anything goes, and as you'll see on the following pages, the scarf you choose really reflects who you are. The scarf makes the woman. You'll notice some of the actresses chose luscious, bold yarns in deep, rich colors, while others chose delicate, subtle effects. Every scarf is different because every woman is different. That's the beauty of knitting your own scarf. It's absolutely you.

Isaac M

Julianna Margulies

"I proudly gave my first knitted scarf to my dad, who actually wore the thing until it started to unravel, at which point he had it framed and hung on his office wall. People thought it was African art."

Julianna Margulies, born and raised in England and New York, appeared in a number of small roles, but it was her riveting performance as Nurse Carol Hathaway on the award-winning television drama series "ER" that launched her career.

Since learning how to knit at the tender age of 5, Julianna has remained enamoured of the craft. "When they asked me to design a project for this book, I tried to find a way to make it interesting by using a novelty yarn," she explains of her design. "I did a simple stockinette stitch and ended up with a soft, luxurious boa-type scarf. But I don't recommend this yarn for beginning knitters. Start with something more malleable and then, as you become more confident in your knitting, give this yarn a try. Be sure to always keep your tension on the loose side; tight stitches are hard to work with and hide the beauty of the yarn."

"MY DAD WORE THE THING UNTIL IT STARTED TO UNRAVEL."

Julianna's scarf

SUGGESTED
MATERIALS
4 skeins Gedifra/KFI
"Techno Hair" (1¾oz/
50g skeins, each
approx 100yd/92m
microfiber) in #09 lt
blue
Size 6 (4mm) knitting
needles

GAUGE
22 sts and 30 rows to
4"/10cm over St st
using size 6 (4mm)
needles

Finished size is
approx 11" x 42"/
28cm x 106.5cm

Cast on 60 sts. Work
in St st (k on RS, p on
WS) for 42"/106.5cm,
or until all yarn is
used up, leaving
enough to bind off.
Bind off.

Rebecca Budig

"My first experience with knitting occurred when I was 14, while on vacation with my friend's family. Her mom, an avid knitter, tried to convince me to concentrate on something other than boys and music. It didn't work."

At Christmas-time in 1993, Rebecca and her three sisters were taught to knit by their mother, and Rebecca is hooked on the craft to this day, buying and storing yarn just like her mother did. "According to my brother-in-law, the first sweater I knit looked like a cover for a space shuttle, so I pawned it off to a friend who's 6'9"," she reveals.

"There is nothing better than sitting around the table in my mother's kitchen, knitting and talking to my mom." When she's not knitting, Rebecca can be seen on the daytime drama "All My Children."

"MY FRIEND'S MOM TRIED TO CONVINCE ME TO CONCENTRATE ON SOMETHING OTHER THAN BOYS AND MUSIC."

Rebecca's scarf

SUGGESTED
MATERIALS
5 skeins Madil/Cascade
Yarns "Boom" (3½oz/
100g skeins, each
approx 22yd/20m wool)
in #206 hot pink (A)
2 skeins Classic Elite
Yarns "La Gran"
(1½oz/42g skeins,
each approx
90yd/82m
mohair/wool/nylon)
in #6571 lt pink (B)
Size 19 (15mm)
knitting needles

GAUGE
6 sts and 8 rows to
4"/10cm over St st
and "Boom" using
size 19 (15mm)
needles

Finished size is
approx 10½" x 75"/
26.5cm x 190cm
(without fringe)

With A, cast on 16
sts. Work in St st (k
on RS, P on WS) and
stripes as foll: *2
rows A, 2 rows B; rep
from * until scarf
measures 75"/190cm,
end with 2 rows A.
With A, bind off.

For fringe, cut one
strand each A and B
each approx
13"/33cm long for
each fringe. Attach 8
fringe along each end
of scarf.

Portia de Rossi

"My mother and grandmother taught me that thinking about the person for whom you are knitting is the most important part of knitting and the secret to being a good knitter."

Born and raised in Melbourne, Australia, Portia was in law school at the University of Melbourne when director John Duigan encouraged her to audition for a low-budget comedy called *Sirens*, in which she starred opposite Hugh Grant, Sam Neill and Elle McPherson. Although she has appeared in various other films, including *Scream II, Who Is Cletis Tout?* (opposite Richard Dreyfuss and Christian Slater), *Women in Film* and *Stigmata,* it was her role as infamous ice queen Nelle Porter on the television series "Ally McBeal" that won her mainstream popularity.

"THINKING ABOUT THE PERSON FOR WHOM YOU ARE KNITTING IS THE MOST IMPORTANT PART."

SUGGESTED
MATERIALS
2 skeins Colinette
Yarns/Unique Kolours
"Point 5" (3½oz/100g
skeins, each approx
54yd/50m wool) in
#99 ice
Size 17 (12.75mm)
knitting needles

GAUGE
8 sts and 11 rows to
4"/10cm over garter
st using size 17
(12.75mm) needles

Finished size is
approx 3" x 100"/
7.5cm x 254cm

Cast on 6 sts. Work
in garter st (k every
row) for 100"/254cm.
Bind off.

Eartha Kitt

With an illustrious career in theater, film, television and the recording industry, Eartha Kitt gives new meaning to the word "versatility." Born in the South and raised in Harlem, the sultry chanteuse began her career as a dancer in the early 1950s. Shortly after, she landed a role in the Broadway production "New Faces of 1952," where she wooed audience members with her rendition of "Monotonous." In the mid-Sixties, her portrayal of Catwoman on the TV series "Batman" made her a favorite of teenagers nationwide.

Highly accomplished, sophisticated and still entertaining legions of fans, Eartha is one of only a handful of performers to be nominated twice for both a Tony and Grammy as well as for an Emmy. Eartha is also the national spokesperson for Project on Growing, which teaches homeless people how to grow their own food.

Eartha began knitting with leftover yarn from her needlepoint projects, making small bears stuffed with old, torn stockings. Restless and eager to keep busy, she often knits at home in front of the TV or during rehearsals.

"I CAN'T STAND TO WASTE ANYTHING—KNITTING IS THE PERFECT WAY TO USE UP ALL MY SCRAP YARN."

SUGGESTED
MATERIALS
12 skeins Elsa
Williams/JCA
"Tapestry Yarn"
(.52oz/15g skeins,
each approx 40yd/
36m wool) in #611
loden
Size 8 (5mm) knitting
needles

GAUGE
16 sts and 30 rows to
4"/10cm over garter
st using size 8 (5mm)
needles

Finished size is
approx 11" x 48"/
28cm x 122cm

Cast on 44 sts. Work
in garter st (k every
row) for 48"/122cm.
Bind off.

Bridget Moynahan

Born in Binghamton, New York, model/actress Bridget Moynahan has posed for *Glamour* and *Vogue* magazines and has appeared in such films as *Coyote Ugly*, *Serendipity* and *The Sum of All Fears*. Hairstylist Jennifer O'Halleron, whom Moynahan met on the set of *The Recruit*, taught her to knit only a year ago; she learned quickly and admits to having an addiction for the craft. "I brought my favorite scarf to a few knitting gurus and they helped me copy the pattern. The scarf I made for this book is a hybrid scarf/hat or scarf/handwarmer."

"IT'S A GREAT WAY TO FILL THE DOWN TIME ON A MOVIE SET."

Bridget's scarf

SUGGESTED
MATERIALS
5 skeins Anny Blatt
"Rustique" (1¾oz/
50g skeins, each
approx 64yd/58m
wool) each in #507
rouge (A) and #427
orchide (B)
Size 10½ (6.5mm)
knitting needles

GAUGE
15 sts and 18 rows to
4"/10cm over St st
using size 10½
(6.5mm) needles

Finished size is
approx 14½" x 81"/
37cm x 205.5cm

With A, cast on 54
sts. Work in St st (k
on RS, p on WS) and
stripes as foll:
18"/46cm (or 80 rows)
A, 9"/23cm (or 40
rows) B, 9"/23cm (or
40 rows) A, 9"/23cm
(or 40 rows) B. Work
next 40 rows as foll:
[2 rows A, 2 rows B]
10 times. Cont St st
stripes as foll:

9"/23cm (or 40 rows)
A, 9"/23cm (or 40
rows) B, 9"/23cm (or
40 rows) A, 18"/46cm
(or 80 rows) B. Bind
off with B.

To finish, fold first
18"/46cm stripe at
one end in half to WS
and sew in place,
leaving center 20 sts
unsewn for pocket.
Work other end of
scarf in same way.
For fringe, cut strands
of each color approx
18"/46cm long. Using
2 strands of each
color, attach 8 fringe
evenly along each
folded edge of scarf.

Leslie Bibb

"The first time I laid eyes on a pair of needles and yarn, I remember feeling a bit overwhelmed. How would I transform this long strand of wool into a cozy scarf using these pointy long sticks?"

Leslie, best known for her starring role on the television series "Popular," has appeared on NBC's "ER" and can soon be seen as the lead in the ABC drama "Lines of Defense." Her film credits include *The Young Unknowns*, *See Spot Run* and *The Skulls*. Leslie began knitting a few years ago on the set of "Popular," after the show's costume designer gave her a knitting kit—a pair of needles and luscious wool yarn—for her birthday. "She knew how bored I was on the set and thought knitting would be the perfect hobby, but it all seemed so daunting! She reassured me that the huge crayon-like needles were the way to go, because they would discourage me from getting frustrated and throwing this fabulous birthday gift out the window of my trailer." She was right. After having to start over only three times because of dropped stitches, Leslie was able to knit her first scarf. "To this day, it's still my favorite."

"HOW WOULD I TRANSFORM THIS LONG STRAND OF WOOL INTO A COZY SCARF?"

Leslie's scarf

SUGGESTED MATERIALS
6 skeins GGH/ Muench Yarns "Aspen" (1¾oz/50g skeins, each approx 63yd/58m wool) in #20 navy (MC) 1 skein each in #30 lt blue (A) and #5 burgundy (B)
Size 11 (8mm) knitting needles

GAUGE
11 sts and 22 rows to 4"/10cm over garter st using size 11 (8mm) needles

Finished size is approx 8½" x 55"/ 21.5cm x 139.5cm

With MC, cast on 24 sts. Work in garter st (k every row) for 30 rows. Change to A and cont in garter st for 10 rows. Change to B and cont in garter st for 6 rows. Change to A and cont in garter st for 10 rows. Change to MC and cont in garter st for 190 rows. Change to A and cont in garter st for 10 rows. Change to B and cont in garter st for 6 rows. Change to A and cont in garter st for 10 rows. Change to MC and cont in garter st for 30 rows. Piece measures approx 55"/139.5cm from beg. Bind off.

For pockets, make 2 pieces as foll:
With MC, cast on 14 sts. K 1 row.
Next row: P2, k10, p2. Rep last row 16 times more. Bind off.
Sew one pocket at each end, centered in MC stripe. Cut a short length of B, tie in a bow and sew in center at top of pocket.

Tracey Gold

"As a mother, it is such a joy to knit cute little hats and scarves for my two sons, and as an actress there is so much down time on a set that a project is greatly appreciated."

Inspired by a good friend, Tracey took up knitting two years ago and has discovered the joys of creating something meaningful with her own hands for her little boys.

Most recognized for her role as Carol Seaver on the Eighties' TV sitcom "Growing Pains," Tracey has appeared in more than thirty made-for-television movies, written a book and spoken extensively about her battle with an eating disorder. She lives with her husband and two children in California.

"IT IS SUCH A JOY TO KNIT CUTE LITTLE HATS AND SCARVES FOR MY TWO SONS."

Tracey's scarf

SUGGESTED
MATERIALS
4 skeins Tahki
Yarns/Tahki•Stacy
Charles, Inc. "Baby"
(3½oz/100g skeins,
each approx
60yd/55m wool)
in #33 navy
Size 19 (15mm)
knitting needles

GAUGE
6 sts and 12 rows to
4"/10cm over garter
st using size 19
(15mm) needles

Finished size is
approx 12½" x 54"/
31.5cm x 137cm

Cast on 19 sts. Work
in garter st (k every
row) for 54"/137cm.
Bind off.

Laura Leighton

"This scarf is the first thing I've ever knit, and I was so happy knowing that it would be included in the book and ultimately benefit AmFAR."

"My mom tried to teach me to knit on several occasions when I was a kid," says Laura, "but I was never inspired to make anything in particular." But last fall, while working on a film project in Vancouver, Canada, Laura witnessed a few women preparing for the winter by knitting hats on the set. A few weekends later, she flew back to Los Angeles and visited a local yarn store. "I was completely blown away by all the beautiful textures and colors," she exclaims.

Asked to contribute to this book, she bought as much yarn as she could and had her mom teach her, once and for all, how to knit. Laura—who appeared on "Melrose Place" and "Beverly Hills 90210"—says that knitting is a great way to spend time with friends when she's not working or taking care of her three children. She and her husband, actor Doug Savant, live in Los Angeles.

"THIS SCARF IS THE FIRST THING I'VE EVER KNIT."

Laura's scarf

approx 116yd/106m angora/wool) in #454 poupre (B)
1 skein Trendsetter Yarns "Perla" (.70oz/20g skeins, each approx 60yd/54m polyester) in #69 antique rose (C)
1 skein Gedifra/KFI "Techno Hair" (1¾oz/50g skeins, each approx 99yd/90m polyamide) in #9641 red (D)
Size 13 (9mm) knitting needles

GAUGE
12 sts and 8 rows to 4"/10cm over pat st and 1 strand A & B held tog using size 13 (9mm) needles

SUGGESTED MATERIALS
2 skeins Anny Blatt "Victoria" (1¾oz/50g skeins, each approx 109yd/100m polyamide) in #454 poupre (A)
2 skeins Anny Blatt "Angora Super" (⅞oz/25g skeins, each

from * to end.
Row 8: Knit, dropping extra wrapped sts.
Rows 9-10: Knit.
Row 11: Rep row 5.
Row 12: Rep row 6.
Rep rows 3-12 for pat st.

With 1 strand each C and D held tog, cast on 15 sts. Work in garter st (k every row) for 4"/10cm. Change to 1 strand each A and B held tog and work in pat st until scarf measures approx 60"/152.5cm from beg, end with a pat row 12. Change to 1 strand each C and D and work in garter st for 4"/10cm. Bind off.

Finished size is approx 5" x 64"/ 12.5cm x 162.5cm

PATTERN STITCH
Rows 1-6: Knit.
Row 7 (RS): *K1 wrapping yarn twice around needle; rep

Jennifer Beals

"After meeting Steven Tyler, one of my all-time favorite fashion icons, at a concert, I knit him an 8-foot-long red chenille scarf, which I didn't think was good enough, so I kept it for myself. I am still anguishing over what type of scarf to knit for him."

After finding success as a steelworker-turned-dancer in *Flashdance*, Jennifer returned to Yale to complete her degree in American Literature. She has appeared in many notable films, including Artisan Entertainment's critically acclaimed *Rodger Dodger*, winner of the 2002 Best Feature Narrative at the Tribeca Film Festival. *In the Soup*, Grand Jury prize winner at the Sundance Film Festival (1992); *Devil in a Blue Dress* opposite Denzel Washington; and the VH-1 movie "They Shoot Divas, Don't They." She has also starred in several made-for-television movies and the series "Nothing Sacred," opposite Kevin Anderson.

"AFTER MEETING STEVEN TYLER… I KNIT HIM AN 8-FOOT-LONG RED CHENILLE SCARF."

Jennifer's scarf

SUGGESTED
MATERIALS
2 skeins Trendsetter
Yarns "Blossom"
(1¾oz/50g skeins,
each approx 96yd/
84m) in #1161 burgundy
Size 13 (9mm)
knitting needles

GAUGE
10 sts and 14 rows to
4"/10cm over garter
st using size 13
(9mm) needles

Finished size is
approx 4" x 96"/10cm
x 244cm

Cast on 10 sts. Work
in garter st (k every
row) for 96"/244cm.
Bind off.

Courtney Thorne-Smith

"My grandmother taught me to knit when I was a little girl. I picked it up again five years ago and I've been knitting happily ever since."

Courtney studied at the Ensemble Theatre Company in northern California before landing a recurring role on "L.A. Law," as Harry Hamlin's "Laker Girl" girlfriend. By 1992, she was playing the tormented character Alison Parker on Melrose Place, which was followed by the role as Georgia Thomas in the critically acclaimed dramatic series "Ally McBeal." She eventually became a spokeswoman for Almay cosmetics. Today, Courtney lives in Los Angeles and stars in the TV comedy "According to Jim" with Jim Belushi.

"MY GRANDMOTHER TAUGHT ME TO KNIT WHEN I WAS A LITTLE GIRL."

SUGGESTED MATERIALS

1 skein Berroco, Inc. "Pleasure" (1¾oz/50g skeins, each approx 130yd/117m merino/angora) each in #8650 runway black (A), #8631 rich blue (B), #8616 emotion (C) and #8614 soft blue (D)

Size 10 (6mm) knitting needles

GAUGE

16 sts and 24 rows to 4"/10cm over St st using size 10 (6mm) needles

Finished size is approx 4" x 91"/10cm x 231cm

With A, cast on 16 sts. Work in St st (k on RS, p on WS) in foll stripes: 7"/17.5cm each A, B, C, D, C, B, A, B, C, D, C, B, A. Bind off. Note: Edges will roll at the sides.

Rosario Dawson

Known as Rosie to friends and family, the New York-born actress was discovered by director Larry Clark while hanging out outside her tenement building back in 1995. Although her career is still young, Rosie has appeared in several independent and blockbuster films, including *He Got Game*, *Josie and the Pussycats*, *Men in Black 2* and *25th Hour*. It was during some downtime on the set of *The Rundown* that the costume designer taught Rosie to knit. Since then, she always keeps a pair of needles and a ball of yarn in tow.

"I THOUGHT IT WOULD BE GREAT TO MAKE EVERYONE A PERSONAL GIFT FOR THE HOLIDAYS."

Rosario's scarf

SUGGESTED
MATERIALS
2 skeins Sirdar/KFI
"Snowflake Chunky"
(1¾oz/50g skeins,
each approx
137yd/126m
polyester) in #382
cream
Size 15 (10mm)
knitting needles

GAUGE
8 sts and 14 rows to
4"/10cm over garter
st using size 15
(10mm) needles

Finished size is
approx 15" x 60"/
38cm x 152cm

Cast on 30 sts. Work
in garter st (k every
row) until piece
measures 60"/152cm
from beg. Bind off.

Nora Dunn

A "Saturday Night Live" alumna, Nora Dunn has also starred in the comedies *Working Girl*, *Bulworth* and *The Three Kings*. After her friend gave her a pair of needles and a ball of yarn one Christmas, Nora was prompted to "tune up [her] technique" by heading off to the yarn shop of the stars, La Knitterie Parisienne, where she fell in love with the textures, hands and colors of the yarns. "I don't expect or aspire to knit as well as proprietor and knitting guru Edith Eig, but she has offered tremendous inspiration," raves Nora. "She knits elegance and designs couture."

"I DON'T SEE KNITTING AS A WAY TO PASS TIME AS MUCH AS A WONDERFUL WAY TO FILL IT."

Nora's scarf

SUGGESTED
MATERIALS
4 skeins Trendsetter
Yarns "Charm"
(.70oz/20g skeins,
each approx
90yd/81m polyester/
tactel) in #114 brown
multi
Size 11 (8mm)
knitting needles

GAUGE
14 sts and 16 rows to
4"/10cm over garter
st using size 11
(8mm) needles

Finished size is
approx 10" x 54"/
25.5cm x 137cm

Cast on 35 sts. Work
in garter st (k every
row) for 54"/137cm.
Bind off.

Jennie Garth

"Knitting is a link to my heritage, and I will pass this hobby on to my daughters, with love."

Jennie's foray into acting began with her role as teen dream Kelly Taylor on "Beverly Hills 90210," earning her recognition among teenagers worldwide. More than a decade later, Jennie has starred in numerous television series and movies. Currently she can be seen on the network sitcom "What I Like About You."

Off camera, Jennie works for various causes. Lending her name to various PETA-sponsored initiatives, she's an advocate for animal rights and was presented with the organization's "Live and Let Live" award. She has also supported the NO-ADdiction™ Campaign, a non-profit organization that works hand in hand with celebrities to prevent drug and alcohol use among high school students. But what Jennie enjoys most of all is spending time with her husband and their two daughters on their farm in the Santa Ynez Valley.

"I WILL PASS THIS HOBBY ON TO MY DAUGHTERS, WITH LOVE."

Jennie's scarf

SUGGESTED
MATERIALS
2 skeins Colinette
Yarns/Unique Kolours
"Point 5" (3½oz/100g
skeins, each approx
54yd/50m wool) in
#124 celadon
Size 17 (12.75mm)
knitting needles

GAUGE
8 sts and 11 rows to
4"/10cm over garter
st using size 17
(12.75mm) needles

Finished size is
approx 6" x 50"/
15.5cm x 127cm
(without fringe)

Cast on 12 sts. Work
in garter st (k every
row) for 50"/127cm.
Bind off.

For fringe cut four
strands of yarn each
approx 11"/28cm
long for each fringe.
Attach four sets of
fringe at each end
of scarf.

Ricki Lake

"Home sick with the flu, I knit this little scarf. It's not my best, but it's the thought that counts!"

Veteran talk show host Ricki Lake, who entertained moviegoers with her memorable performances in *Hairspray* and *Cry Baby*, has been knitting since she was in junior high school. "My mother, sister and I learned the craft at Saturday-morning knitting class," she tells us. "I started out knitting scarves and have graduated to sweaters, hats, blankets and booties for my two boys." A few months ago, a friend called and asked her to do this book, telling her she had one day to finish her project!

"IT'S NOT MY BEST, BUT IT'S THE THOUGHT THAT COUNTS!"

Ricki's scarf

SUGGESTED
MATERIALS
2 skeins Tahki Yarns/
Tahki•Stacy Charles,
Inc. "Baby" (3½oz/
100g skeins, each
approx 60yd/55m
wool) in #33 navy
Size 17 (12.75mm)
knitting needles

GAUGE
9 sts and 18 rows to
4"/10cm over garter
st using size 17
(12.75mm) needles

Finished size is
approx 5½" x 28"/
14cm x 71cm

Cast on 12 sts. Work
in garter st (k every
row) for 28"/71cm.
Bind off.

Ever Carradine

"When I was 6, I went to an artsy type school where all the kids learn to knit in the first grade. I think it took the whole year, but the first thing I managed to make was an oven mitt."

Daughter of actor Robert Carradine, Ever entered Lewis & Clark College as an anthropology and sociology major, but changed her ways and returned to her roots, switching her major to theater. Ever has been a series regular on such memorable television shows as "Once & Again," "Veronica's Closet" and "Party of Five." She currently stars in the FX series "Lucky" opposite John Corbett. Ever's feature film credits include *The Bubble Boy*, *Jay and Silent Bob Strike Back* and *The Right Stuff*.

"IT TOOK THE WHOLE YEAR, BUT THE FIRST THING I MANAGED TO MAKE WAS AN OVEN MITT."

Ever's scarf

SUGGESTED
MATERIALS
2 skeins On Line/KFl
"Scala" (1¾oz/50g
skeins, each approx
71yd/65m tactel/
nylon) in #06 green
(MC)
1 skein Anny Blatt,
"Rustique" (1¾oz/50g
skeins, each approx
64yd/58m wool) in
#250 multi (CC)
Sizes 10½ and 13 (6.5
and 9mm) knitting
needles

GAUGE
12 sts and 18 rows to
4"/10cm over garter
st and "Scala" using
size 13 (9mm) needles

Finished size is
approx 4" x 50"/
10cm x 127cm

With smaller needles
and CC, cast on 12
sts. Work in St st (k
on RS, p on WS) for
4"/10cm. Change to
larger needles and
MC and work in
garter st (k every row)
until piece measures
46"/117cm from beg.
Change to smaller
needles and CC and
work in St st for
4"/10cm. Bind off.

To finish, fold St st
edge at ends of scarf
in half so that knit
side is showing and
sew in place.

Tekitha

"Knitting has been an invaluable addition to my life: it relaxes my mind and keeps me focused on the moment."

A member of the New York City-based hip-hop ensemble Wu-Tang Family, R&B vocalist Tekitha has contributed to "Wu All Stars" "Soul in the Hole," Ghostface Killah's classic "All That I Got Is You" and Cappadonna's "Pump Your Fist." She recently learned how to knit following a chance encounter with Abra Edelman. "I was inspired by the idea of making sweaters for my 2-year-old daughter," she says.

"IT RELAXES MY MIND AND KEEPS ME FOCUSED ON THE MOMENT."

Tekitha's scarf

SUGGESTED
MATERIALS
1 skein Colinette
Yarns/Unique Kolours
"Tagliatelle"
(3½oz/100g skeins,
each approx 173yd/
160m wool/nylon)
in #134 jubilee
Size 10 (6mm)
knitting needles

GAUGE
13 sts and 24 rows to
4"/10cm over garter
st using size 10
(6mm) needles

Finished size is
approx 5" x 60"/
12.5cm x 152cm

Cast on 18 sts. Work
in garter st (k every
row) for 60"/152cm,
or until yarn runs out.
Bind off.

Lauren Ambrose

Lauren Ambrose learned how to knit last year on the set of *Six Feet Under*. Kathy from the wardrobe department, who Lauren says is an amazing craftsperson, had the patience to teach her during stolen moments between shots and scenes.

"I knew Hollywood's rich knitting history and its reputation for turning some of its renowned divas on to the craft. The mysterious skill, with all its fun equipment, always fascinated me," Lauren says. She still can't believe that she can make something to wear and keep her warm out of a ball of yarn. Knitting makes her feel productive ("and like an old-fashioned lady!"). Last year, she made some scarves—some for presents and some for wearing—but by summertime she lost her passion for working with a lapful of wool. However, she became newly inspired by a recent trip to Iceland, where, Lauren says, "knitting and wool are not only all the rage but also a way of life—sheep outnumber people four to one! When I returned home to a less formidable climate, I decided to make this scarf. It reminds me of Iceland. It is young and fun like Reykjavik. I think it looks like something Bjork or some other hip Icelander might wear to keep warm." Made to be worn countless different ways, this scarf reminds her of the rainbows in the mist at the double waterfall at Gulfoss.

"KNITTING AND WOOL ARE NOT ONLY ALL THE RAGE BUT ALSO A WAY OF LIFE…"

Lauren's scarf

SUGGESTED
MATERIALS
1 skein Naturwolle/
Muench Yarns
"Multicolor" (3½oz/
100g skeins, each
approx 108yd/100m
wool) in #61
regenbogen (rainbow)
Size 10 (6mm)
knitting needles

GAUGE
12 sts and 10 rows to
4"/10cm over garter
st using size 10
(6mm) needles

Finished size is
approx 2½" x 100"/
6.5cm x 254cm
(without fringe)

Cast on 7 sts. Work
in garter st (k every
row) for 100"/254cm.
Bind off.

For fringe, cut strands
of yarn each approx
12"/30.5cm long.
Attach 7 sets of
fringe at each end
of scarf.

Shelley Morrison

"When I was 6, my mother took me on a vacation to the Catskills, where I started playing with her knitting. Instead of scolding me, she sat me down and taught me to knit so I would respect her work."

Known today for her role as the feisty Salvadoran housekeeper on the hit television sitcom "Will & Grace," Shelley has appeared in more than sixty-five plays, 150 television series and fifteen feature films over a 40-year career. In the early 1960s, she directed plays at the Edinburgh Fringe Festival and became one of Los Angeles's youngest theatrical producers (credits include "Sweet Bird of Youth" and "Hamlet"). Shelley is also known for her active involvement in community work.

"INSTEAD OF SCOLDING ME, MY MOM SAT ME DOWN AND TAUGHT ME TO KNIT."

SUGGESTED
MATERIALS
1 skein Cherry Tree
Hill "Silky Pastels"
(4oz/115g skeins,
each approx 280yd/
252m rayon/silk) in
peacock
Size 8 (5mm) knitting
needles

GAUGE
20 sts and 20 rows to
4"/10cm over k5, p5
rib (slightly stretched)
using size 8 (5mm)
needles

Finished size is
approx 5" x 60"/
12.5cm x 152cm

Cast on 25 sts.
Row 1 (RS): K5, *p5,
k5; rep from * to end.
Row 2: P5, *k5, p5;
rep from * to end.
Rep rows 1 and 2 for
k5, p5 rib until scarf
measures 60"/152cm.
Bind off in rib.

Shiri Appleby

"I love doing something creative between shots. I find knitting very therapeutic in that my hands are moving as quickly as my mind."

Shiri Appleby's rise to recognition began with roles in the television drama "Roswell" and the film *Swimfan*. She learned to knit at 20 but confesses that knitting felt awkward at first because she was already accustomed to crocheting. "But once I got the hang of it, I felt an overwhelming sense of accomplishment," she says. "Since then, I have used my skills on many occasions. If I've been fighting with my boyfriend, I pick up my sticks. When I am shopping and can't find anything else to spend my money on, I head over to the local yarn store. When someone I know is expecting a child or has a birthday coming up, I make a blanket or a beautiful scarf. Everyone appreciates a thoughtful handmade gift."

"I LOVE DOING SOMETHING CREATIVE BETWEEN SHOTS."

Shiri's scarf

SUGGESTED
MATERIALS
3 skeins Rowan Yarns
"Biggy Print" (3½oz/
100g skeins, each
approx 32yd/29m
wool) in #253 joker
Size 35 (19mm)
knitting needles

GAUGE
6 sts and 7 rows to
4"/10cm over garter
st using size 35
(19mm) needles

Finished size is
approx 4" x 102"/
10cm x 259cm

Cast on 6 sts. Work
in garter st (k every
row) for 102"/259cm.
Bind off.

Vanna White

Television celebrity Vanna White may owe her fame to the long-running game show, "Wheel of Fortune," but much of her success is contributed to other projects, including commericial endorsements, publication of her autobiography *Vanna Speaks* and even a Learjet charter business. Vanna has been crocheting since she was a little girl, and recently published a series of crochet books featuring her own designs. "My grandmother taught me the chain stitch," she tells us. "Twenty years later, I was sitting in the makeup chair at 'Wheel of Fortune' and my hair dresser was crocheting a baby blanket. I started watching her and picked it up again." In spite of all the changes in her life, one thing has remained constant: her love for crochet.

"THE INTERESTING THING IS, I AM RIGHT-HANDED BUT CROCHET WITH MY LEFT HAND."

Vanna's scarf

SUGGESTED MATERIALS

6 skeins Lion Brand Yarn Co., "MicroSpun" (2½oz/70g skeins, each approx 168yd/155m acrylic) in #186 mango
Size I (5.5mm) crochet hook

GAUGE

16 sts and 8 rows to 4"/10cm over dc pat using size I (5.5mm) hook

Finished size is approx 22" x 60"/56cm x 152cm

Ch 92. Work in dc pat as foll:

Row 1: Dc in 4th ch from hook and in next 4 ch, *skip next 2 ch, dc in next 4 ch, 3 dc in next ch, dc in next 4 ch; rep from * to last ch, 2 dc in last ch. Ch 3, turn (counts as first dc of next row).

Row 2: Dc in first 5 dc, *skip next 2 dc, dc in next 4 dc, 3 dc in next dc, dc in next 4 dc; rep from * to last dc, 2 dc in last st. Ch 3, turn (counts as first dc of next row).

Rep row 2 for dc pat until scarf measures approx 60"/152cm. Fasten off.

Daryl Hannah

"Knitting is meditative and calming, and you always wind up with some tangible satisfaction."

Her performances as a painted android in *Blade Runner* and the guileless mermaid in *Splash* catapulted Hollywood bombshell Daryl Hannah to stardom, leading her to appear in more than forty films in a career that has spanned more than two decades.

The actress estimates that she's stitched seven or eight scarves in her knitting career. This one, which she calls *chévere* (a Colombian word for "all good things"), took only two days to complete. "I striped the scarf using various yarns—embroidery, thread, eyelash, ribbon—to create an interesting texture, look and hand." She adds, "Half way through making the scarf, I lost one the needles so I had to use a Sharpie™, which is about the size of an #11 needle."

"KNITTING IS MEDITATIVE AND CALMING."

Daryl's scarf

SUGGESTED MATERIALS

1 skein Prism "Wild Stuff" (85g-114g each approx 150yd/135m mohair blend) in antique
Note: If "Wild Stuff" is not available, listed below are some yarn suggestions.

1 skein Judi & Co. "¼" Rayon Ribbon" (1¾oz/50g skeins, rayon) in ecru
1 skein Trendsetter Yarns "Aura" (1¾oz/50g skeins, each approx 95yd/86m nylon) in white
1 skein Trendsetter Yarns "Flora" (.70oz/20g skeins, each approx 72yd/65m viscose/polyester) in white
1 skein Trendsetter Yarns "Eyelash" (.70oz/20g skeins, each approx 80yd/72m polyester) in white
1 skein Trendsetter Yarns "Voila" (1¾oz/50g skeins, each approx 180yd/162m nylon) in white
1 skein Trendsetter Yarns "Perla" (.70oz/20g skeins, each approx 77yd/70m polyester) in #22 white
Size 13 (9mm) knitting needles

GAUGE

22 sts to 4"/10cm over garter st using size 13 (9mm) needles
Note: Due to the variety of yarn weights used in this scarf, the gauge will vary.

Finished size is approx 2½ - 4"/6.5 - 10cm wide (depending on yarn) x 66"/167.5cm long (without fringe)

Cast on 14 sts. Work in garter st (k every row) varying the yarns (if not using "Wild Stuff") every 1½"/4cm to 3"/7.5cm as desired, until scarf measures approx 66"/175cm, or desired length. Bind off.

For fringe, cut strands of ribbon yarn approx 28"/71cm long. Using 2 strands for each fringe, attach 6 fringe at each end of scarf.

Parker Posey

"I knit when I'm working, because it puts my mind in a relaxed meditative place and instigates good conversation."

Her dynamic approach to acting and innate comic sensibility have led Parker to star in numerous films, including *Personal Velocity*, *Best in Show*, *The Anniversary Party*, *Scream 3* and *Waiting for Guffman*. A fan of crafts in general, Parker had always wanted to learn to knit. "Granny would knit shawls, and I always appreciated the effort and time it took to make something." Parker used chunky needles and a yarn from Halifax, Nova Scotia, to create this scarf. "I bought a big stash of yarn in various colors that would look good together. I often knit with two or three strands to make the scarf cozy and original looking."

"IT PUTS MY MIND IN A RELAXED MEDITATIVE PLACE."

Parker's scarf

SUGGESTED
MATERIALS
Note: The yarns used
in this scarf are not
available. Use any
hand-dyed bulky
Bouclé yarn together
with a light-weight
mohair in two
different colors
to achieve the
finished look.
Size 19 (15mm)
knitting needles

GAUGE
6 sts and 8 rows to
4"/10cm over St st
and 1 strand bouclé
plus 1 strand mohair
held tog using size 19
(15mm) needles

Finished size is
approx 16" x 52"/
40.5cm x 132cm

With 1 strand of each
yarn held tog, cast on
24 sts. Work in St st
(k on RS, p on WS)
for 40"/101.5cm.
Work in reverse St st
(p on RS, k on WS)
for 12"/30.5cm.
Bind off.

Justine Bateman

"I knit because I'm addicted, I suppose. The vast selection of yarns and colors available seduce me, and the ideas I envision haunt me until I manifest them. I can't not knit."

Searching for an activity to occupy her mind, Justine began knitting out of necessity. "I took to knitting and crocheting very easily and began making my own patterns for everything from hats and bikinis to ponchos," she says. "The response was so overwhelming, I began a design business, and today I have a hand-knit couture and ready-to-wear line."

Best known for her role as Mallory Keaton in the long-running sitcom "Family Ties," Bateman's "Parfait" scarf, featured here, is worked in merino wool, two colors of mohair and a variegated chunky yarn to create the layered effect of the dessert after which it is named. "It will curl naturally to give you a skinny scarf look, but if you prefer a wide, flat look, knit in garter stitch. Knitters of any skill level can achieve this complex-looking scarf. It's the yarn that makes it look so good."

"I KNIT BECAUSE I'M ADDICTED, I SUPPOSE."

Justine's scarf

1 skein Filatura di Crosa/Tahki•Stacy Charles, Inc. "Butterfly" (1¾oz/50g skeins, each approx 192yd/177m mohair/acrylic in #402 blue (E)
1 skein Trendsetter Yarns "Mohair" (1¾oz/50g skeins, each approx 164yd/148m mohair/acrylic) in #457 lt green (F)
Size 17 (12.75mm) knitting needles

GAUGE
8 sts and 13 rows to 4"/10cm over pat st and "Point 5" using size 17 (12.75mm) needles

Note: When changing colors, always beg a new color on a RS row.

With A, cast on 24 sts. Work in pat st in foll stripes:
3"/7.5cm A,
5½"/14cm D,
4"/10cm F,
2½"/6.5cm B,
3"/7.5cm C,
4½"/11.5cm E,
3½"/9cm D,
12½"/31.5cm F,
3"/7.5cm B,
2½"/6.5cm C,
3½"/9cm E,
2"/5cm B,
5"/12.5cm D,
2½"/6.5cm F,
3"/7.5cm A.
Bind off with A.

SUGGESTED MATERIALS
1 skein Colinette Yarns/Unique Kolours "Point 5" (3½oz/100g skeins, each approx 54yd/50m wool) each in purple (A) and morocco (B)
1 skein Anny Blatt "Merinos" (1¾oz/50g skeins, each approx 137yd/127m wool) in #19 aurore (C)
1 skein Pingouin/Colorado Yarns "Illusion" (3½oz/100g skeins, each approx 54yd/50m wool) in #103 lavender (D)

Finished size is approx 12" x 60"/ 30.5cm x 127cm

PATTERN STITCH
Row 1 (RS): Knit.
Row 2: *K1, p1; rep from * to end.
Rep rows 1 and 2 for pat st.

Marissa
Ribisi

Marissa's introduction to knitting began with her first heartbreak, at 14. "I was convinced it was the end of the world," she reminisces. "To save me and the rest of the family from my misery, my stepmother suggested I take up a hobby like knitting." Marissa was reluctant at first, doubting her own attention span. "I wondered how I could hold onto a ball of yarn and needles when I couldn't even manage a teenage boy. But my stepmother was persistent and touted the therapeutic benefits. I wasn't sure what 'therapeutic' meant, but I knew that I needed it." Within days, Marissa mastered the craft and quickly graduated from making potholders and scarves to blankets and sweaters. "I now have about twelve sweaters and more than thirty scarves and hats. Most of all, I have my heart back."

Her film credits include *Dazed and Confused*, *Pleasantville* and *According to Spencer*.

"MISTAKES ARE GOOD—A SCARF SHOULD LOOK LIKE YOU MADE IT, NOT LIKE YOU BOUGHT IT AT THE GAP."

SUGGESTED
MATERIALS
Small amounts of
several different
leftover yarns in a
similar weight
Recommended
needle size for
chosen yarns

GAUGE
Recommended gauge
for chosen yarns

Finished size is
approx 10" x 72"/
25.5cm x 183cm

Cast on 30 sts (more
or less for desired
width) and work in
garter st (k every row)
in varying stripe pat,
until scarf measures
72"/183cm, or
desired length.
Bind off.

Rosie Perez

"I learned to crochet when I was 9. We were so poor back then, we had to do something to keep ourselves occupied."

The Brooklyn-born actress, who began her career as a choreographer, is best known for her portrayals of loquacious spitfires in such urban-life films as *Do the Right Thing* and *White Men Can't Jump.* But it was Rosie's restrained performance as a plane-crash survivor in the 1993 film *Fearless* that wrangled her an Oscar nomination for Best Supporting Actress. Her latest endeavor: the lead in the Broadway revival of *Frankie and Johnny in the Clair de Lune.*

For Rosie, who learned to crochet at an early age, the craft is a source of relaxation. "If I am really stressed, I can finish an entire scarf in one day."

"WE WERE SO POOR BACK THEN, WE HAD TO DO SOMETHING TO KEEP US OCCUPIED."

SUGGESTED
MATERIALS
4 skeins Tahki Yarns/
Tahki•Stacy Charles,
Inc. "Baby" (3½oz/
100g skeins, each
approx 60yd/55m
wool) in #20 red
Size Q (16mm)
crochet hook

GAUGE
5 dc to 4"/10cm and
5 rows to 6"/15,5cm
over dc pat using size
Q (16mm) hook

Finished size is
approx 6" x
91"/15.5cm x 231cm

Ch 118.
Row 1: Dc in 4th ch
from hook and in
each ch to end. Ch 3,
turn.
Row 2: Sk first dc,
working into back
loops only, dc in each
dc to end, dc in top of
ch-3. Ch 3, turn.
Rows 3-5: Rep row 2.
Fasten off.

the yarns used in this book

Several of the yarns used to make the scarves in this book have been discontinued or are not available in the U.S. We have recommended yarns that are available at the time of printing and will most closely resemble the pictured scarf. However, there are no set measurements for the finished size of a scarf. It can be as long and wide as you want. It can also be made in any type of yarn. While we have given a recommended yarn, needle size and gauge, feel free to use whatever yarn and needle size you wish. Perhaps you have some leftover yarn from a previous project, or you find only a few balls of a fabulous yarn in your travels. Simply cast on and knit until you run out of yarn. The options are endless.

abbreviations

approx approximately

beg begin, begins or beginning

CC contrasting color

ch chain

cm centimeters

cont continue

dc double crochet

foll follow, follows or following

g grams

k knit

m meter

MC main color

mm millimeter

oz ounces

p purl

pat pattern

rep repeat

RS right side

sk skip

st(s) stitch(es)

St st stockinette stitch

tog together

WS wrong side

yd yards

acknowledgements

Editorial Director
Trisha Malcolm

Art Director
Chi Ling Moy

Page Layout
Doug Rosensweig

Copy
Leslie Barber
Michelle Lo

Instructions
Carla Scott
Karen Greenwald
Veronica Manno

Photography
David Jakle
Jack Deutsch Studios
Dorian Caster
Sam Handel

Still Photography Stylist
Laura Maffeo

Book Managers
Cara Beckerich
Theresa McKeon

Production Manager
David Joinnides

**President and Publisher,
Sixth&Spring Books**
Art Joinnides

Photo Credits

David Jakle
(pp. 9, 13, 16, 19, 20, 23, 24, 27, 28, 31,
32, 35, 36, 39, 40, 43, 44, 47, 48, 51, 52,
55, 56, 59, 60, 63, 64, 67, 68, 71, 72, 75,
76, 79, 80, 83, 84, 87, 88, 95, 96, 99, 100,
103, 104, 107, 108, 111, 112)

Jack Deutsch
(pp. 5, 12, 17, 21, 25, 29, 33, 37, 41, 45, 49,
53, 57, 61, 65, 69, 73, 77, 81, 85, 89, 93, 97,
101, 105, 109, 113, 114, 115, 116, 117)

Dorian Caster
(pp. 55, 56 and 119)

Sam Handel
(pp. 79 and 80)

Pages 91 and 92
Released by permission from
(Vanna's Favorite Crochet Gifts), Oxmoor House
To order book call: 1800-643-8030

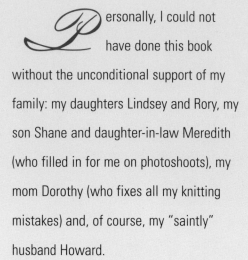

Personally, I could not have done this book without the unconditional support of my family: my daughters Lindsey and Rory, my son Shane and daughter-in-law Meredith (who filled in for me on photoshoots), my mom Dorothy (who fixes all my knitting mistakes) and, of course, my "saintly" husband Howard.

Many people contributed their time, services and facilities, and without them this book would not have been possible. I'd like to thank Gretchen Vater (Pier 59 Studios), Bryan Suckut (Clear Lounge), Susan Mischer (Knit Café), Will Blochinger (Axis Studios), Mark McKenna (Herb Ritts Studio), Argyle Hotel and Nicole Landers (Smart Water).

A special thank you to Theresa McKeon for not giving up until this book was published.

I would also like to express my gratitude to the assistants, stylists and hair and makeup artists: Daniel Erdman, Alexander Becker, Colleen Conway, Jennifer Duryani, Victor Alegria, Diana Schmidtke and Jared Raskind. A very special thank you goes out to makeup artist Gina Brooke, who is not only talented but selfless in her work with all the celebrities.

This book would not have existed without the assistance from the agents, managers and publicists: Gay Ribisi, Steve Siebert, Dan Ortega, Bonnie Leidke, Brian Young, Bradley Frank, Michael Garnett, Steve Dontanville, Nicole Perez, Greg Siegel, Evan Hainey, Jim Broutman, Joel Rudnick, Daphne Ortiz, Joan Hyler, Randy James, Jamie French, Holly Fussel, Jennifer Pinto, Craig Schneider, Jillian Fowkes, Mike Cohen, Frank Frattaroli, Michelle Boxer and my friend Pamela Segal Adlon.

Our amazing fashion photographer, David Jakle, would like to dedicate these photos to his good friend and mentor Herb Ritts, who generously donated his studio for many of the portraits in this book. Herb saw nothing but absolute beauty in everyone he photographed, and in doing so, we saw the beauty and love in him. Herb brought out the best in everyone. I know he brought out the best in David.

resources

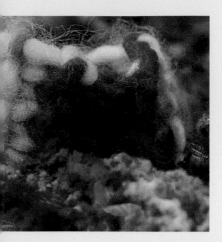

US RESOURCES

Write to the yarn companies listed below for purchasing and mail-order information.

Anny Blatt/Bouton d'Or
7796 Boardwalk
Brighton, MI 48116

Berroco, Inc.
PO Box 367
Uxbridge, MA 01569

Cascade Yarns
1224 Andover Park East
Tukwila, WA 98188

Cherry Tree Hill Yarns
PO Box 659
Barton, VT 05822

Classic Elite Yarns
300 Jackson Street Bldg. #5
Lowell, MA 01852

Colorado Yarns
P.O. Box 217
Colorado Spring, CO 80901

Colinette Yarns
distributed by Unique Kolours

Elsa Williams
distributed by JCA, Inc.

Filatura di Crosa
distributed by Tahki•Stacy Charles, Inc.

GGH
distributed by Muench Yarns

Gedifra
distributed by Knitting Fever, Inc.

JCA
35 Scales Lane
Townsend, MA 01469

Knitting Fever, Inc.
P. O. Box 502
Roosevelt, NY 11575

Lion Brand Yarn Co.
34 West 15th Street
New York, NY 10011

Madil
distributed by Cascade Yarns

Muench Yarns
285 Bel Marin Keys Blvd.
Unit J
Novato, CA 94949-5724

Naturwolle
distributed Muench Yarns

On Line
distributed Knitting Fever, Inc.

Pingouin
distributed Colorado Yarns

Rowan Yarns
4 Townsend West, Suite 8
Nashua, NH 03063

Sirdar
distributed by Knitting Fever, Inc.

Tahki Yarns
distributed by Tahki•Stacy Charles, Inc.

Tahki•Stacy Charles, Inc.
8000 Cooper Ave.
Glendale, NY 11385

Trendsetter Yarns
16745 Saticoy St. #101
Van Nuys, CA 91406

Unique Kolours
1428 Oak Lane
Downingtown, PA 19335

CANADIAN RESOURCES

Write to US resources for mail-order availability of yarns not listed.

Berroco, Inc.
distributed by S. R. Kertzer, Ltd.

Diamond Yarn
9697 St. Laurent
Montreal, PQ H3L 2N1
and
155 Martin Ross, Unit #3
Toronto, ON M3J 2L9

Les Fils Muench
5640 Rue Valcourt
Brossard, PQ J4W 1C5

Rowan Yarns
distributed by Diamond Yarn

S. R. Kertzer, Ltd.
105A Winges Rd.
Woodbridge, ON L4L 6C2